VIRTUAL HISTORY TOURS

Look around a

GREEK TEMPLE

Richard Dargie

ARCTURUS

This edition first published by Arcturus Publishing
Distributed by Black Rabbit Books
123 South Broad Street
Mankato
Minnesota MN 56001

Printed in China

Library of Congress Cataloging-in-Publication Data
Dargie, Richard.
  Look around a Greek temple / by Richard Dargie.
      p. cm. -- (Virtual history tours)
Includes index.
ISBN 978-1-84193-720-5 (alk. paper)
1. Acropolis (Athens, Greece)--Juvenile literature.
2. Temples--Greece--Athens--Juvenile literature.
3. Greece--Civilization--To 146 B.C.--Juvenile literature. I. Title.

DF287.A2D37 2007
938'.5--dc22

                  2007007559

9 8 7 6 5 4 3 2

Series concept: Alex Woolf
Editor and picture researcher: Alex Woolf
Designer: Ian Winton
Illustrator: Phil Gleaves

Picture credits:
Bailey Publishing Associates: 11.
Art Archive: 4 (JFB), 9 (Muzeul de Sarmezegetusa, Romania / Dagli Orti), 10 (Musée du Louvre, Paris / Dagli Orti), 13 (Acropolis Museum, Athens / Dagli Orti), 14 (Dagli Orti), 15 (Acropolis Museum, Athens / Dagli Orti), 17 (Musée du Louvre, Paris / Dagli Orti), 20 (Acropolis Museum, Athens / Dagli Orti), 21 (Museo Civico Orvieto / Dagli Orti), 24 (Musée du Louvre, Paris / Dagli Orti), 27 (Musée du Louvre, Paris / Dagli Orti), 28 (National Archaeological Museum, Athens / Dagli Orti).
Corbis: 6 (Pete Saloutos / zefa), 7 (Christie's Images), 8 (Gianni Dagli Orti), 12 (Werner Forman), 16 (Archivo Iconografico, SA), 18 (Mimmo Jodice), 19 (Gianni Dagli Orti), 22 (Roger Wood), 25 (Gianni Dagli Orti), 26 (Ted Spiegel), 29 (Bettmann).
TopFoto: 23 (AAAC).

CONTENTS

THE ACROPOLIS OF ATHENS

Welcome to ancient Athens! On this tour, you will visit the Acropolis, the heart of the city, where the ancient Athenians built temples to their favorite gods and goddesses. You will visit these temples and see the treasures stored inside. You will also visit the altars and other sacred places on the Acropolis where the citizens of Athens worshipped and held their religious festivals.

The upper city

Almost 4,000 years ago, the first Athenians settled on a high limestone rock that stood more than 300 feet (100 m) above the surrounding plains of Attica in southern Greece. It was a safe place to build a settlement since there were steep cliffs on all sides. The rock was known as the Acropolis, or "upper city." Sometimes it was called the Cecropia after Cecrops, the legendary founder of Athens, who was said to be half man, half serpent.

TOMB OF CECROPS: SEE PAGE 19

Over time, the people of Athens began to build their houses on the lower plains around the Acropolis. The rock became the palace and fortress of the early kings of Athens and a place of safety in times of war. By 500 BCE, it had become a holy place where the Athenians built temples to the gods and kept sacred objects and statues.

Pericles (495–429 BCE) was the leading statesman of Athens during its "golden age" in the fifth century BCE. Under his rule, many temples and monuments were built in the city.

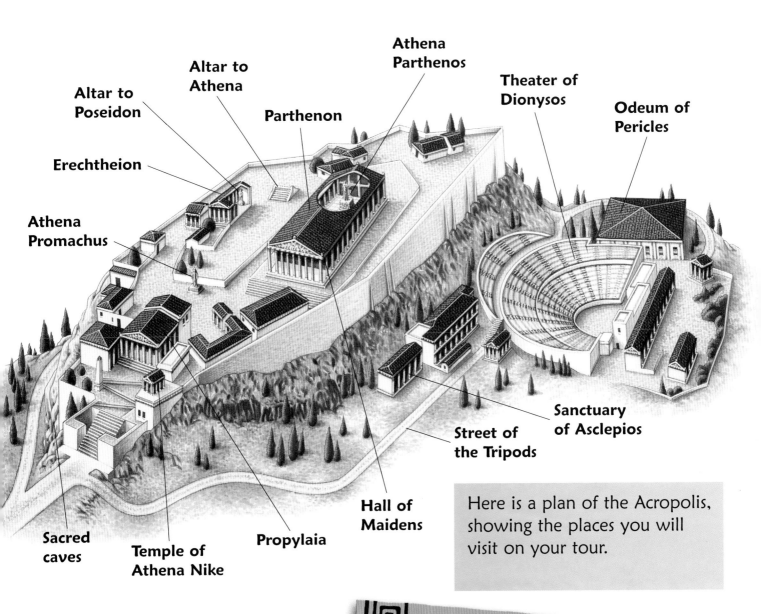

Altar to
Poseidon

Altar to
Athena

Athena
Parthenos

Theater of
Dionysos

Odeum of
Pericles

Parthenon

Erechtheion

Athena
Promachus

Sanctuary
of Asclepios

Street of
the Tripods

Hall of
Maidens

Here is a plan of the Acropolis,
showing the places you will
visit on your tour.

Sacred
caves

Temple of
Athena Nike

Propylaia

The city rebuilt

Between 490 and 479 BCE, the
Athenians fought a long and bitter
war against the mighty Persian
Empire. During that war, the city of
Athens was captured and burned to
the ground. The fine buildings on
the Acropolis were destroyed. After
Athens finally won the war, the
Athenian leader Pericles decided to
celebrate by making the Acropolis
beautiful again.

The historian Plutach describes
the building of the new
Acropolis:

*That which gave most pleasure
and ornament to the city of
Athens, and the greatest
admiration and even astonishment
to all strangers, and that which
now is Greece's only evidence of
her ancient power and wealth,
was his [Pericles's] construction
of the public and sacred buildings.
The materials were stone, brass,
ivory, gold, ebony, cypress wood.*

Life of Pericles, XII–XIII

5

SINGING TO THE GODS

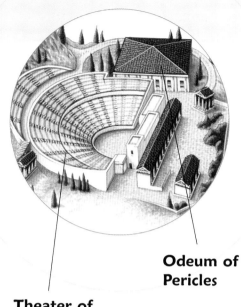

Your tour begins on the Street of the Tripods, which lies below the Acropolis and leads to its only gate. On this street, you will find two buildings. In the Odeum of Pericles you can hear Athenians singing songs about the gods and heroes of Greek myth. In the Theater of Dionysos, you can join an audience of 15,000 spectators watching plays about the gods.

Odeum of Pericles

Theater of Dionysos

Street of the Tripods

The Street of the Tripods was used as a sacred way during religious festivals. The street was lined with shrines that held statues of the gods on bronze tripods. These were

built by the *choregoi*, wealthy Athenians who were in charge of the music and drama contests. Before the contests, the *choregoi* would sacrifice a piglet to purify the theater and lead the performers in a solemn procession.

The Theater of Dionysos was built into the southern slopes of the Acropolis hill. It was the first stone theater built in the ancient world.

The Odeum of Pericles

Sacred songs were performed in the odeum built by Pericles. As a reminder of the Athenian victory over the Persians, this concert hall copied the great pavilion in which the Persian king Xerxes used to sit on his throne. The pillars that held up the roof were made from planks taken from captured Persian ships. The most popular singers and musicians could win prizes of gilded wreaths of wild olives and up to 500 silver drachmas.

Plutarch describes the Odeum:

The odeum, which was arranged internally with many tiers of seats and many pillars and which had a roof made with a circular slope from a single peak, they say was an exact reproduction of the great king's pavilion. Then . . . Pericles got a decree passed that a musical contest be held as part of the Panathenaic festival. He himself was elected manager and prescribed how the contestants must blow the flute or sing, or pluck the zither.

Life of Pericles, XIII.5

PERICLES: SEE PAGES 4–5

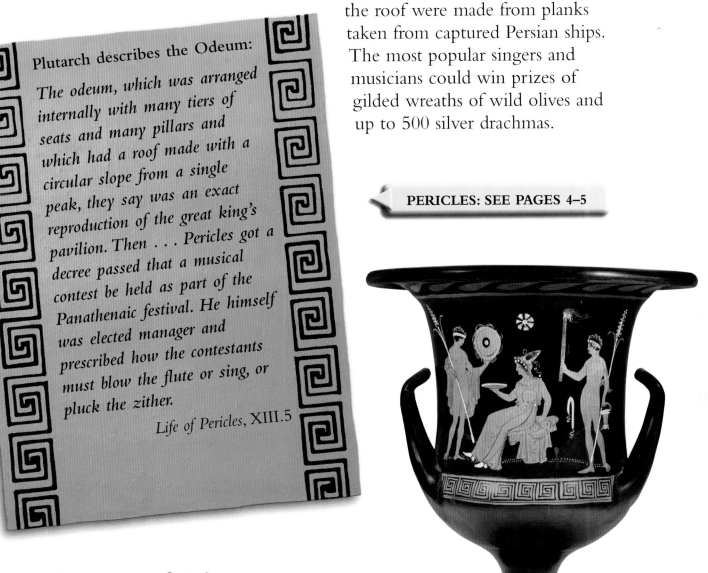

This vase is decorated with a scene from a play by the playwright Euripides. Vases showing scenes from plays were made to commemorate victory in the drama festival.

The Theater of Dionysos

Plays were put on in the theater during January and March as part of the festival of Dionysos, the god of wine and religious mysteries. The Greeks believed that the gods looked down on the theater from the Acropolis and watched the tragedies. These were often sad or shocking plays about the fate of men and women who had angered the gods.

PRAYING FOR HEALTH

Farther along the Street of the Tripods, you can visit the sanctuary of Asclepios, where sick Athenians come to ask Asclepios, the god of medicine, to be healed. You can drink from the spring of healing, which trickles out from a cave in the Acropolis rock, then sleep with the sacred snakes, and the gods will speak to you in your dreams.

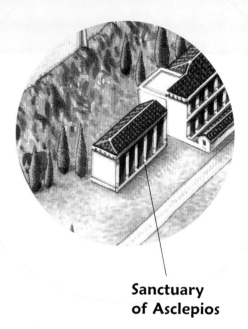

Sanctuary of Asclepios

God of healing

In Greek legend, Asclepios was a doctor and the son of Apollo, god of the sun. Asclepios learned the secrets of medicine from the mythical half man, half horse, Chiron the centaur. Asclepios's shrine, the Asclepeion, was one of the richest temples in Athens. It was decorated with paintings, statues, and valuable objects that were given to the temple by the god's grateful patients.

This stone carving shows the god Asclepios healing one of his patients, attended by his daughters, Hygiene, Medicine, and Healing.

Sacred snakes

Athenians suffering from an illness often visited the shrine of Asclepios in search of a cure. After making a sacrifice to the god, they spent the night sleeping in a room where the sacred snakes of Asclepios were kept. The next morning, the patients described their dreams to the temple priests, who then matched the dream to a suitable ointment or herbal remedy.

This gilded head of Medusa the Gorgon shows the snakes writhing in her hair. One glance from her was said to turn onlookers to stone. The Greeks believed that Athena gave Asclepios Medusa's magical blood.

The historian Apollodorus describes Asclepios's powers:

As a surgeon, Asclepios became so skilled that he not only saved lives but even revived the dead, for he had received from Athena the blood that had coursed through the Gorgon's veins. The left-side portion he used to destroy people, but the right he used for their preservation, which is how he could revive those who had died.

The Library, 2.144

Blood of Medusa

The temple was guarded by a brotherhood of healing priests called the Asclepiadae. They were said to keep a powerful medicine, made from the blood of Medusa the Gorgon, that could bring the dead back to life. The shrine also contained a spring that flowed from a cleft in the rock of the Acropolis. This spring water was also believed to have healing powers.

THE SACRED CAVES

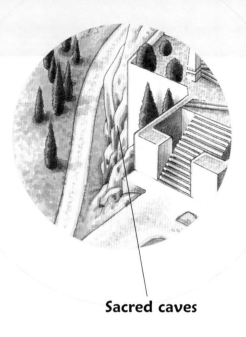

N ow you're at the gateway that takes you up into the Acropolis. Before you go up, look at the caves in the Acropolis rock. Each one is the shrine to a god and has its own legend. From here you can watch the sacred processions making their way up to the Acropolis from the city below. You can also see the massive stones used to build the first walls around the Acropolis.

Sacred caves

Sanctuary of Aglauros

In one cave was the sanctuary of Aglauros, one of three royal sisters in the early days of Athens. The goddess Athena asked the sisters to guard a locked box but ordered them not to open it since it contained a secret. One of the girls opened the box, however. Fearing that angry Athena would punish the whole city, Aglauros threw herself from the cliffs of the Acropolis to save Athens. Each year, the magistrates who ruled Athens visited the cave to take their oaths of loyalty. Sacred processions to the temples of the Acropolis also stopped here to thank the princess for protecting the city.

The massive walls of the Acropolis were built in about 1300 BCE. In later times, Greeks believed they had been built by giants. This vase painting shows Cyclops, the legendary giant, carrying stones to build the Acropolis wall.

10

Shrine to Pan

Near the Acropolis gateway is a cave that was a shrine to Pan, the woodland god. Pan was honored by the Athenians because he had helped the city. When a large Persian army invaded Greece in 490 BCE, the Athenians sent the runner Philippides to raise help from the city of Sparta. Pan appeared to Philippides during his run and promised to help the Athenians. After their victory in the Battle of Marathon, the Athenians left gifts of grain in Pan's sanctuary and held a torch race in his honor every year.

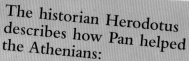

WAR WITH PERSIA: SEE PAGE 5

The historian Herodotus describes how Pan helped the Athenians:

The generals first sent to Sparta the herald Philippides. . . . Pan called out Philippides' name and bade him ask the Athenians why they paid him no attention, though he was of goodwill to the Athenians . . . and would be in the future. When the Athenians became prosperous, they established a sacred precinct of Pan beneath the Acropolis. Ever since that message they honor him with annual sacrifices and a torch race.

Histories, 6.105.1

Pan, the woodland god of shepherds and herdsmen, was half man and half goat. The Athenians left gifts for him in a cave on the Acropolis hill.

GATEWAY TO THE GODS

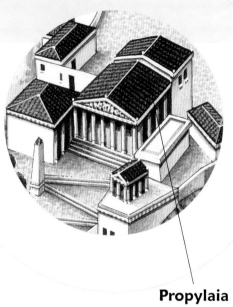

Propylaia

Now you must clamber up the steep flight of steps toward the shimmering white marble gateway at the western edge of the Acropolis. This is the Propylaia, one of the greatest glories of Athens. You will pass through six massive columns that lead to the gates into the sacred area. Look for signs of the ramp used by chariots and to drive up the herds of sacrificial animals.

In 480 BCE, a Persian army captured the Acropolis. The old gate was badly damaged by the Persians, so in 437 BCE, Pericles asked the architect Mnesicles to design a monumental gateway that would show off the wealth of Athens. The Propylaia, which means "before the doors," took five years to build and cost the immense sum of over 2,000 talents.

The great gates of the Propylaia have vanished. Only the columns remain. The columns are made of marble and were built in a simple style called Doric.

Unfinished masterpiece

The Propylaia was used in many religious festivals. Processions stopped here to sacrifice animals to the gods on the Propylaian altar before entering the Acropolis. Many Athenians thought that the Propylaia was the loveliest building in their city. Its roof of deep blue spotted with golden stars was famous throughout Greece. The Propylaia was never finished, however. A long war between Athens and Sparta broke out in 431 BCE, and there was never enough money or workers to finish Mnesicles' masterpiece.

WAR WITH SPARTA: SEE PAGE 15

Traveler and writer Pausanias describes the Propylaia:

There is but one entry to the Acropolis. It affords no other, being precipitous throughout and having a strong wall. The gateway has a roof of white marble, and down to the present day it is unrivaled for the beauty and size of its stones.

Description of Greece, 1.22.4

Guarding the Acropolis

The Propylaia was the only way into the Acropolis. This made it easy for the priests to check who was entering. They could stop anyone who was unclean or who had angered the gods. The guards at the Propylaian gate also made sure that known thieves were prevented from getting access to the treasures inside.

This stone carving shows priests leading bulls to be sacrificed in the Acropolis. Each year, bulls were led here and sacrificed to Athena, Zeus, and Poseidon.

THE TEMPLE OF VICTORY

Just over here above the stairs of the Propylaia is the beautiful temple of Athena Nike, Goddess of Victory. You can walk into the *cella*, or inner chamber, of the temple and marvel at the bronze statue of Athena, created by the gifted sculptor Phidias. Outside again, you can stand on the temple balcony with its frieze of victory statues and look out across the city to the blue Aegean Sea beyond.

Temple of Athena Nike

PROPYLAIA: SEE PAGES 12–13

Broken wings

Athena was the patron goddess of Athens. The city was named after her and had many temples in her honor. The Temple of Athena Nike was used in times of war when the Athenians prayed to the winged goddess for victory over their enemies. In the temple, they even kept a statue of the goddess with her wings deliberately broken off so she could never leave the city and take the hope of victory with her.

The slim, fluted columns of the Athena Nike were built in the graceful Ionic style. The architect Callicrates designed the temple with four columns at the front and the rear.

The temple of Athena Nike was built high on a bastion, or tower, of the old city wall. The Athenians built the temple in 425 BCE when they were fighting Sparta, hoping that the goddess would help them beat their enemy. The temple and its balcony were decorated with images of war and victory. The frieze around the temple walls showed the Athenian army defeating the Persians and their allies in the Battle of Plataea in 479 BCE.

Most of the temple's sculptures are lost, but this stone carving of Athena undoing her sandal has survived. Athenian sculptors such as Phidias were skilled at showing the draped folds of Athena's garments.

The playwright Aristophanes writes a prayer to the goddess Athena:

Holy . . . Athena, our guardian queen, ruling over the holiest land, a land poetic famed and strong, first in battle and first in song, a land whose equal was never seen. . . . Bring with thee the maiden bright, She who greets us in every fight—Victory!

The Knights, 551–94

Temple priestess

The citizens of Athens chose the temple priestess in an election. Her job was to guard the statues of Athena and to make sacrifices to the goddess on the altar of Nike at the temple door. Hundreds of animals were slaughtered in the Acropolis every year, but the very best animal was given to the temple of Nike. The priestess had the right to keep the leg meat and the leather from all the sacrificed animals.

STATUES OF ATHENA: SEE PAGES 18, 21, AND 28–29

THE HOLY OF HOLIES

To the north of the Acropolis, you will find the temple of Athena Polias, protector of the city. Some call it the Erechtheion after an early king of Athens. Note the beautiful statues of maidens holding up the porch. Before you go in, you will see the altar to Zeus the Most High. And look at the yard at the other end—that is where they keep the holy snake of Cecrops, legendary founder of the city.

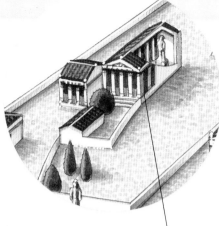

Erechtheion

TOMB OF CECROPS:
SEE PAGE 19

Athena and Poseidon

The Erechtheion was the holiest place in Athens. Many gods were worshipped here, but especially Athena and Poseidon, the god of the sea. According to legend, the two gods competed for control of Athens. Poseidon threw his trident at the Acropolis and water burst from the rock. Unfortunately, it was undrinkable seawater. Athena touched the rock with her spear and an olive tree began to grow, so the grateful Athenians named the city after her.

ALTAR TO POSEIDON:
SEE PAGES 18 AND 19

The Erechtheion has an unusual shape since it was built over several old shrines. Six figures of maidens, called *caryatids*, hold up the side porch.

16

Strong women

The Erechtheion replaced a much older temple destroyed by the Persians. It was begun in 421 BCE and finished in 406 BCE. Instead of columns, the southern porch was held up by six strong female figures called *corai*, or maidens. The figures were sometimes called *caryatids* because they resembled the women of Carya in southern Greece, famed for their strength and beauty.

ALTAR TO ZEUS: SEE PAGES 19, 20 AND 21

King Erechtheus

Outside the temple entrance was an altar where cakes were left every day to Zeus. A frieze on the temple wall told the story of the birth of Erechtheus, one of the earliest Athenian kings, who was buried under the temple. He was said to have founded the annual Panathenaic festival of songs, plays, and games to honor Athena.

Herodotus describes the legend of Athena and Poseidon:

On the Acropolis is a spot sacred to Erechtheus, and within it is an olive tree and a spring of salt water. According to local legend they were put there by Poseidon and Athena when they contended for possession of the land. . . . Now, this olive was destroyed by fire together with the rest of the sanctuary by the Persians. On the very next day, a new shoot eighteen inches long had sprung from the stump.

Herodotus VIII, 55

This vase painting shows Athena (on the left) competing with Poseidon for control of the city, while other gods look on.

INSIDE THE ERECHTHEION

As you enter the first chamber of the Erechtheion, you will see an altar to Poseidon. Straight ahead, in the second chamber, is the saltwater well made by Poseidon and the marks that his trident left on the rock. The walls of the chamber are lined with shelves groaning with Persian treasure. And here, in a walled niche, is the statue of Athena Polias, the most sacred object in the city.

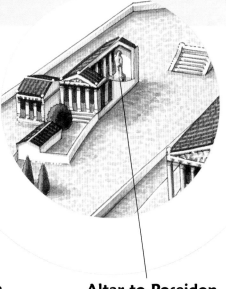

Altar to Poseidon

From the heavens

The small wooden statue of Athena inside the Erechtheion was greatly revered by the Athenians, who believed that it had fallen from the heavens. Each year, in a festival called the Plynteria, the statue was carefully carried to the sea to be washed by priestesses. Then a procession carried a fine woolen *peplos*, or dress, into the temple as a gift for Athena. The *peplos* was made by Athenian noblewomen, helped by young maiden priestesses.

The inside of the Erechtheion was the most sacred place in Athens. Only marble survives today, but in ancient times, the temple was decorated with colorful paintings and rich cloth hangings.

Everlasting lamp

Beside the goddess was a special lamp that amazed the ancient travelers who saw it. Crafted by the sculptor Callimachus, the lamp burned every day and every night but only needed filling with oil once a year. The lamp was crowned by a giant bronze palm that gathered the smoke and carried it through the roof of the temple.

Many other gods were worshipped in the Erechtheion. There were altars to Zeus, Poseidon, and Hephaistos, the god of blacksmiths. The temple also held the tomb of Cecrops. Athenians believed that two sets of marks inside the temple were made by a thunderbolt from Zeus and by Poseidon's trident. The sound of waves breaking on the shore could be heard coming from Poseidon's well, even though the Acropolis is 5 miles (8 km) from the sea.

Plutarch describes an arrival in Athens during the Plynteria:

Alcibiades put into harbor on the day when the festival of the Plynteria of the goddess Athena was being celebrated. The priestesses celebrate these rites in strict secrecy, removing the robes of the goddess and covering up her image. The Athenians regard this as the unluckiest of all days for business of any sort. The goddess, therefore, did not appear to welcome Alcibiades but rather to veil herself from him and repel him.

Alcibiades 34

Zeus, the king of the Greek gods, was worshipped at a special altar inside the Erechtheion. This statue shows him about to throw a thunderbolt.

SHRINES, STATUES, AND ALTARS

Here at the center of the Acropolis are the great altars to Athena and Zeus, where herds of cattle are sacrificed to the gods. Visit on a feast day and the priests will give you gifts of cooked meat from the altar and a goblet of wine. Walk around between the temples and you will see dozens of statues of gods and heroes from Greek mythology.

Altar to Athena

Cleansing ceremonies

All of the Acropolis was holy to ancient Athenians. Today the site is mostly empty, but in ancient times, it was packed with sacred temples, shrines, altars, and statues. Only people who had undertaken cleansing ceremonies were allowed to enter, and unclean beasts were forbidden. Athenians were horrified in 300 BCE when a dog got into the Acropolis and defiled the temples of Athena.

This early Greek statue shows a calf being carried to sacrifice inside the Acropolis. The blood, bones, and hide of sacrificed animals were given to the gods. The meat was usually eaten by the Athenians.

The Hecatomb

At the highest point of the Acropolis were altars to Athena and Zeus. Every year, a special sacrifice of a hundred oxen, the Hecatomb, took place here. If the gods were thought to be angry with Athens, the animals were quickly burned on the altar so that only the gods could enjoy them. If the gods were pleased, the animals were cooked slowly and their meat shared out among the citizens. The winner of a torch race had the privilege of lighting the altar fire.

Plutarch recalls the simpler festivals of earlier times:

In the old days the festival of Dionysos consisted of a procession organized in a popular and cheerful style: a jar of wine and a vine, then someone dragging a he-goat, another followed carrying a wicker basket of raisins. But now these things are ignored . . . when gold vessels are borne along and expensive costumes and teams of horses and masks.

Plutarch 3, 527

Athena Promachus

Nearby stood a giant bronze statue of Athena Promachus, or Athena the Warrior, that was over 33 feet (10 m) high. Everyone in the city could see the statue, and the sun glinting on the goddess's golden spear helped to guide Athenian sailors far out at sea. The statue took its sculptor, Phidias, several years to build and cost 700 talents. Other statues included the legendary hero Theseus, who killed the fierce bull-monster the Minotaur.

Athena was almost always shown wearing a battle helmet and carrying a javelin or spear.

THE PARTHENON

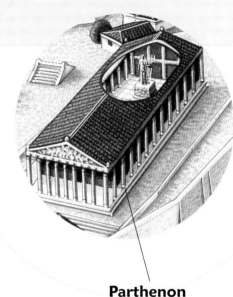

Parthenon

Towering over all the other buildings on the Acropolis is the Great Temple of Athena, which some call the Parthenon. You can see it from every part of the city. Walk around to the eastern end and you will find the main entrance to the temple. Above the doorway is a magnificent pediment, or triangle of sculptures, that tell the story of Athena's birth.

In 448 BCE, Pericles asked the sculptor Phidias and the architects Callicrates and Ictinus to design a new temple to Athena. This great temple took 15 years to complete and came to be known as the Temple of Athena Parthenos, or Athena the Maiden.

The Parthenon is almost 230 feet (70 m) long and 102 feet (31 m) wide. Its 46 columns are over 33 feet (10 m) high. It is made of a beautiful white stone called Pentelic marble.

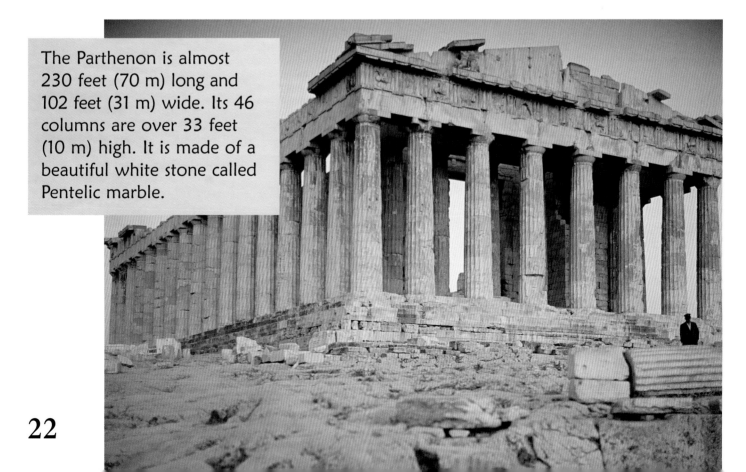

Marble statues

With 46 columns over 33 feet (10 m) high, the Parthenon was easily the largest temple on the Acropolis. Above the main entrance at the eastern end was one of the masterpieces of Phidias, a triangular pediment filled with marble statues, each one over 10 feet (3 m) high. These marbles told the story of the unusual birth of Athena. Hephaistos, the god of blacksmiths, smashed Zeus's skull with an ax. Athena sprang from her father's head, fully armed and wearing a warrior's helmet.

ALTAR TO HEPHAISTOS:
SEE PAGE 19

This vase painting shows the birth of Athena. The newly born goddess springs from an ax wound in her father, Zeus's, skull. The god Hephaistos stands nearby, holding his ax.

The poet Homer describes the birth of Athena:

From his awful head Zeus himself bore her dressed in warlike arms of flashing gold, and awe seized the gods as they gazed. But Athena sprang quickly from the immortal head and stood before Zeus . . . shaking a sharp spear. Great Olympus began to reel fearfully at the might of the bright-eyed goddess and the earth round about cried dreadfully and the sea was moved and tossed with dark waves.

Homeric Hymn 28, 3–12

The western door of the Parthenon was crowned with another pediment of huge statues by Phidias. These told the story of the struggle between Athena and Poseidon for control of the city. In the center was a bronze image of the olive tree that Athena gifted to the Athenians.

THE TREASURES OF ATHENA

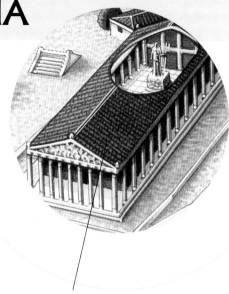

Hall of Maidens

Come around to the western end of the Parthenon and walk in through the great wooden doors under the fabulous statues of Athena and Poseidon. You can see the thunderbolt sent by Zeus to calm Poseidon when he lost the contest. Now you are standing outside the Hall of Maidens, the treasury of Athena, where the wealth of Athens is kept safe.

Procession and prizes

During the Panathenaic festival, a holy procession to the Acropolis carried a sacred *peplos* (dress) to Athena. The procession stopped on the steps at the western end of the Parthenon. Here prizes were awarded by priestesses to the competitors who had won the singing, drama, and athletics contests. The prizes were amphorae, or decorated vases, filled with sacred olive oil, and wreaths of myrtle and laurel.

PANATHENAIC FESTIVAL: SEE PAGE 27

This vase painting shows the amphorae, or clay vases, filled with precious oils that were given to successful sportsmen in the Panathenaic Games. A priestess of Athena presents the gifts to the winning athlete.

Hall of Maidens

The western chamber of the temple was called the Parthenon, or Hall of Maidens. Over time, the name Parthenon came to mean the whole temple. Only officials called the Treasurers of Athena were allowed into this locked room. At the start of their term of office, they had to count the valuables in the treasury and list them on marble tablets. When they gave up their office, the treasures were checked against the list. If anything was missing, the treasurers could be charged with theft and exiled.

Items on a list from the Parthenon treasury from 414 BCE:

Six Persian daggers overlaid with gold, a gold-plated helmet, 13 shields of gilt wood, unmarked gold of seven drachmas weight, 12 stalks of gold wheat, gilt monster figures, a silver mask of 116 drachmas weight, an ivory-inlaid table, gold earrings set with stones of 21 drachmas weight, a gilt lyre, 138 silver vessels, an incense burner of gilt wood, and six golden wreaths.

The treasures of Athena were a mix of jewelry, precious vases, and richly decorated furniture. Some of the treasures had been won by Athenian armies in wars and taken as booty. Other items in the treasury were given to the temple by rich Athenians who wanted help from the goddess. The gifts were kept in the chamber in wooden cupboards and put on display on marble shelves.

This gold dagger probably belonged to a Persian nobleman. The Athenians captured many fine weapons like this in their wars with the Persians and stored them in the Parthenon treasury.

GODS, GIANTS, AND HEROES

Athena Parthenos

Walk around outside the Parthenon and you will see the amazing sculptures that Phidias designed to decorate the temple. Above the columns, you can see a band of sculptures that tell stories from Greek legend and history. Around the inner wall is a long sculpted frieze that shows the people of Athens making their way to the Acropolis to worship Athena.

Legends in stone

The outside of the Parthenon was decorated with bands of lively sculptures running around all four sides of the building. Above the columns, the sculptures told famous stories from Greek legend and history. The eastern side showed the battle between the gods of Olympus, led by Zeus, and the Giants who fought against them for control of the heavens. The sculptures on the western end told of an ancient war between the Greeks and the Amazons, a tribe of fierce female warriors from Asia.

The skill of Phidias and his fellow sculptors brought the ancient legends of the Greeks to life on the Parthenon frieze. This carving shows a battle between civilized men and savage centaurs.

The sculptures on the southern flank described the battle between a Greek people called the Lapiths and the centaurs, mythical creatures that were half human, half horse. The northern sculptures showed scenes from the 10-year war that the Greeks fought against the Trojans to win back their kidnapped queen Helen.

This part of the Parthenon frieze shows the Athenian noblewomen in charge of the sacred *peplos* of Athena. The carving was originally covered in blue and gold paint.

The Panathenaea

Around the inner part of the temple ran a sculpture frieze. This showed the people of Athens taking part in the Great Panathenaea, the special festival in honor of Athena that took place every four years. The frieze shows the procession that walked from the city to the Acropolis carrying the new *peplos* for the statue of the goddess. It showed the ordinary people of Athens—citizens, immigrants, women, youths, and maidens—preparing to honor Athena. Behind the city magistrates were musicians and worshippers carrying trays and baskets with gifts for the goddess and leading cattle to sacrifice.

The Roman writer Quintilian praises the talents of Phidias:

Phidias is regarded as more gifted in his representation of gods . . . and indeed for gold and ivory statues he is without a peer, as he would in truth be, even if he had produced nothing in this material beyond his Athena at Athens . . . so perfectly did the majesty of the work give the impression of godhead.

Quintilian 12, 10.9

STATUE OF ATHENA POLIAS: SEE PAGE 18

ATHENA PARTHENOS

Chamber of Athena

Now enter the eastern chamber of the Parthenon. This is the *cella*, or chamber of Athena. Look up and marvel at the giant statue of Athena Parthenos, one of the largest in the ancient world and the finest work of the sculptor Phidias. It is wooden inside but has been completely covered in precious ivory and plates of beaten gold.

Phidias's downfall

Pericles asked Phidias to build a vast statue of the goddess in the eastern chamber of the temple. This statue was over 33 feet (10 m) high and towered above the worshippers who stood before her. It was one of the most impressive statues in the ancient world. However, Phidias's great work made him many enemies since other artists were jealous of his skill. He was accused of stealing some of the ivory and gold meant for the statue, and he died soon afterward in prison.

The great statue of Athena Parthenos was lost after classical times. Only smaller Roman copies such as this one survive. Athena rests her hand on a pillar and holds a winged Nike, symbol of victory.

Power and wisdom

Everything about the statue was intended to remind the viewer of the power and wisdom of Athena and her city. Athena stood like a warrior, holding a spear in her left hand while a shield lay against her leg. On her head was a triple-crested helmet topped with a sphinx, symbol of wisdom, and with a winged horse at each side. In her right hand, she held a winged Nike, or statue of victory. Athena's shield was decorated with scenes of her battles against the Giants and shows her helping the Greeks against the Amazons.

> **TEMPLE OF ATHENA NIKE: SEE PAGES 14–15**

This 19th-century reconstruction of the chamber of Athena shows how the giant statue of the goddess might have looked, towering over the humans below.

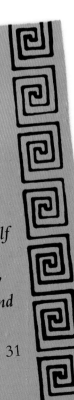

Plutarch explains why Phidias was envied:

The reputation of his works was what brought envy upon Phidias; especially where he represents the fight against the Amazons upon the shield of the goddess Athena, he introduced a likeness of himself holding up a great stone with both hands and put in a very fine representation of his friend Pericles fighting an Amazon.

Pericles 31

Lost wonder

Phidias's great statue was lost over time and has disappeared. Sadly, many of the temples and treasures of the Acropolis have also been lost, but enough remains to show us that it was one of the wonders of the ancient world.

TIMELINE

All dates are BCE.

c. 2000	The first major settlements are built on the Acropolis.
c. 1400	A royal palace is built on the Acropolis.
c. 1300	The Athenians raise the Cyclopean Walls.
c. 600	The first temple to Athena is built on the Acropolis.
566	The Panathenaic festival is first celebrated.
490	The Athenians defeat the Persians at the Battle of Marathon.
480	The Persians destroy the temples on the Acropolis.
480	The Athenians destroy the Persian fleet at Salamis.
479	The Athenians defeat the Persians at the Battle of Plataea.
c. 470	The Theater of Dionysos is built.
468	The walls and gates of the Acropolis are repaired.
c. 455	The giant bronze statue of Athena is erected by Phidias.
c. 450	The Odeum of Pericles is constructed.
448	Pericles decides to rebuild the temples on the Acropolis.
c. 447	Construction of the Parthenon begins.
c. 438	The Parthenon is completed.
437	The building of the Propylaia begins.
432	The decoration of the Parthenon is completed.
431	War with Sparta stops work on the Propylaia.
430	Phidias the sculptor dies.
429	Pericles dies.
425	Construction of the Temple of Athena Nike begins.
415	The Temple of Athena Nike is completed after a break caused by the war with Sparta.
421	Construction of the Erechtheion begins.
420	The Asclepeion is constructed.
406	The Erechtheion is completed.
338	The golden age of Athens ends with defeat by the Macedonians.

GLOSSARY

booty Money and treasure taken by a victorious army in wartime.

cleft A narrow crack or opening in a cliff.

decree An order by a king or leader that must be obeyed.

defile Make something unclean, impure, and unholy.

drachma An Athenian coin. A workman earned one drachma each day.

frieze A piece of decoration, often painted or in sculpture, running along a wall.

incense A substance made of plants and oil, burned in temples to make a pleasant smell.

Gorgon A mythical monster. Looking at a Gorgon turned the observer to stone.

laurel A tough, shiny, evergreen plant that was shaped into a crown or wreath.

limestone A soft, easily worked white stone.

lyre An ancient U-shaped harp.

magistrate An official who helped to govern Athens and carry out the law.

myrtle A sweet-smelling, shiny leaf used in sacred ceremonies.

patron A special protector who looks after a city or a country.

pavilion A large tent used by generals when on campaign with their armies.

pediment A triangular part at the top of a building, often decorated with statues.

peplos A loose-fitting dress worn by women in ancient Greece.

precipitous Very steep.

sanctuary A holy place devoted to a particular god or goddess where runaways could claim protection from the law.

shrine A very small temple or other holy place, usually with a statue of a god or goddess.

talent A unit of gold or silver of very great value.

trident A spear with three sharp points, like a giant fork.

tripod A support or stand with three legs.

wreath Circlets or crowns made from shaped laurel and other plants.

zither A small wooden instrument played by plucking its strings.

FURTHER INFORMATION

Books

Chrisp, Peter. *Great Buildings: The Parthenon*. Wayland, 1996.

MacDonald, Fiona. *I Wonder Why the Greeks Built Temples: and Other Questions About Ancient Greece*. Kingfisher Books, 1997.

Malam, John. *An Ancient Greek Temple*. Book House, 2005.

Malam, John. *Pinpoints: An Ancient Greek Temple*. Wayland, 2001.

Shuter, Jane. *Picture the Past: Life in a Greek Temple*. Heinemann Library, 2005.

Websites

www.culture.gr/2/21/211/21101a/e211aa01.html
This is the official Acropolis website of the Hellenic Ministry of Culture. It is informative and well illustrated.

www.acropolis360.com/
This website provides the visitor with a virtual photographic tour of the Acropolis ruins.

www.goddess-athena.org/
This well-illustrated website is devoted to all aspects of archaeological and historical evidence relating to the worship of the goddess Athena.

INDEX